MADI COFFEE RECIPES

JANE ROMSEY

Published by Fat Dog Publishing LLC in 2016

First edition; First printing
© 2016 Jane Romsey
All rights reserved. No part of this book may be reproduced or transmitted in any form or by any means, including but not limited to information storage and retrieval systems, electronic, mechanical, photocopy, recording, etc. without written permission from the copyright holder.

ISBN: 978-1-943828-11-1

Contents

Boozy Espresso Balls —44
Cappuccino Cheesecake Pie with Pecan Sauce —42
Chocolate Coffee Ruin Cake —12
Chocolate Espresso Cake —28
Chocolate Espresso Muffins —34
Chocolate Fudge Frosting —49
Coffee Banana Nut Muffins —32
Coffee Buttercream Frosting —46
Coffee Carrot Cake —14
Coffee & Cream Cake —10
Coffee Cream Cheese Frosting —45
Coffee Creme Brownies —38
Coffee Fruit Cake —36
Coffee Fudge Frosting —48
Coffee Ginger Muffins —19
Coffee Glace Icing —51
Coffee Macarons —24
Coffee Madeira Cake —33
Coffee Pecan Muffins —26
Coffee Rice Pudding — 37
Crunchy Coffee Bars — 27
Espresso Brownies —16
Espresso Buttercream Frosting —47
Espresso Choc Banana Bread —22
Jane's Special Espresso Martini — 52
Mocha Cookies —41
Mocha Mayonnaise Cake —18
Mocha Sour Cream Frosting —50
Moist Coffee Cake —30
Walnut Coffee Sandwich —20

Introduction

I wouldn't say I'm a coffee addict by any means, but I do really love the flavor of coffee and enjoy an extra strong cappuccino every morning. So I'm a sucker for anything made with coffee, especially cake. When I first moved to the United States from England many years ago, I bought a slice of coffee cake only to discover that there was not a drop of coffee in it and it's only called coffee cake because it's served with coffee!

In this book is a collection of cake, muffin, brownie and dessert recipes all made with coffee. You can eat them with coffee, or tea, or wine, beer or even milk if you like. Or, my very favorite Espresso Martini, my own recipe that I brew up every Christmas.

I hope you enjoy these treats as much as I do.

Jane

Conversion Charts

If you would prefer to use ounces I have added the conversions here. I didn't want to include the conversion in each recipe as it would make the ingredient lists very cluttered. As there aren't many it's very easy to learn the equivalent cups in ounces.

Weights vs. Measures
The most accurate way to bake is to weigh ingredients.
-Professional bakers weigh ingredients.
-In Europe, home bakers weigh ingredients.
-American home bakers measure.

Oven temperatures

F	C	GAS
225	110	¼
250	130	½
275	140	1
300	150	2
325	170	3
350	180	4
375	190	5
400	200	6
425	220	7
450	230	8
475	240	9

Baking Measurements English & Metric

How to accurately measure dry ingredients.

Weighing ingredients is the most accurate method. If measuring with utensils, always use standard dry measurement cups and spoons.

Stir flour, powdered sugar, cocoa etc., until light and loose.

Sift first if recipe instructs to do so.

Use a tablespoon to lightly spoon into the cup until it is heaped up above the edge.

Don't shake or tap to settle flour.

Level off with the straightedge, not flat side of a spatula.

Remember: Each type of flour or ingredient will weigh a different amount per cup. Unless they are "standardized" measuring cups and spoons, they may vary depending on where they are bought.

Dry Measurement
Pinch = 1/16 teaspoon
Dash = 1/8 teaspoon or less
1 teaspoon = 1/3 tablespoon = 5 ml
3 teaspoons = 1 tablespoon = 15 ml
2 tablespoons = 1/8 cup or 1 ounce
4 tablespoons =1/4 cup
5 tablespoons + 1 teaspoon = 1/3 cup
10 tablespoons + 2 teaspoons = 2/3 cup

8 tablespoons = 1/2 cup
1/2 cup + 2 tablespoons = 5/8 cup
12 tablespoons OR 1/2 c + 1/4 c = 3/4 cup
16 tablespoons = 1 cup
Zest of 1/2 lemon rind = 3/8 oz = 1 tablespoon
Zest of 1/4 orange rind = 3/8 oz = 1 tablespoon

Fluid Measurement

Measure liquids in a liquid measuring cup or beaker.
Set the cup or beaker on a flat surface.
Look at the amount at eye level.

1 cup = 8 fl.ounces = 237 ml
2 cups = 1 pint = 16 oz = 473 ml (0.473 liters)
4 cups = 2 pints = 1 qt = 32 fl. oz.= 946 ml (0.946 liters)
4 quarts = 1 gallon

oz. = ounce or ounces
c. = cup
T. = tbsp.= tablespoon
t. = tsp. = teaspoon
g = gram or grams = 0.035 oz lb. = pound = 454 grams
1 ounce = 28.35 grams
1 liter = 1.06 quarts

Ingredient Weight Equivalents
Stir, spoon and level method of measuring dry ingredients used.

Dry Ingredients
All-purpose flour 1 cup = 4 oz = 112g
Cake flour 1 cup = 3.75 oz = 105g
Bran, dry (not cereal) 1 cup = 2 oz = 56g

Bread flour 1 cup = 4.5 oz = 126g
Soy flour (defatted) 1 cup = 4 oz = 112g
Cornmeal 1 cup = 5.33 oz = 150g
Cocoa (baking) 1/4 cup = 1 oz = 28g
Rolled oats 1 cup = 3.25 oz = 90g
Dry milk 1 cup = 3.5 oz = 98g
Granulated sugar 1tsp.= 4g 1c.= 7 oz=196g. 1lb. = 2c.
Brown sugar, packed 1cup = 7 oz=196g 1lb.= 2 1/4 cup
Powdered (6X) sugar, sifted 1c=4 oz=112g. 1lb = 4 1/2 c
Raisins 1 cup = 5 1/4 oz
Fresh or frozen blueberries 1 cup = 5.25 oz = 147g
Chopped nuts 1 cup = 3.75 oz = 105g
Vegetable shortening 1 cup = 6.75 oz
Butter 1 cup = 8 oz = 2 sticks
Baking Soda 1 tsp = 1/16 oz = 4.7g
Baking powder 1 tsp. = 1/8 oz = 3.5g
Salt 1 tsp. = 1/6 oz = 4.7g
Cinnamon, cloves, nutmeg 1 Tbsp. = 1/12 oz = 2.3g
Active dry or instant yeast 1pkg.= 2 1/4 tsp. = 7g

Fluid Ingredients
Honey 1 cup = 12 oz
Maple Syrup 1 cup = 11.5 oz
Vegetable oil 1 cup = 7 oz
Molasses 1 cup = 11 oz
Water or Vinegar 1 cup = 8 oz
Milk 1 cup = 8.5 oz
Whole egg, large* 1 egg = 1 2/3 oz = 10 per lb.
Fluid eggs 1 cup = 5 eggs = 8 oz
Egg white 1 white = 1 oz = 8 oz whites = 1 cup = 8 oz
Egg Yolk 1 yolk = ~2/3oz 12 yolks = 8 oz = 1 cup
*Large eggs are standard size used for home baking

Coffee & Cream Cake

2 cups all purpose flour
2 cups sugar
¼ teaspoon salt
2 sticks butter
4 tablespoons instant coffee dissolved in 1 cup boiling water, or, 1 cup strong brewed coffee
½ cup buttermilk
2 eggs
1 teaspoon baking soda
2 teaspoons vanilla

Icing
1½ sticks butter
1lb icing/confectioners' sugar
2 tablespoons instant coffee
¼ teaspoon salt
4 tablespoons heavy cream

Preheat oven to 350F.
Grease and flour or line two 7 or 8 inch round baking pans.

Mix sugar, flour and salt together in large bowl.

Melt 2 sticks of butter in a pan over medium-low heat. Once butter has melted, add coffee to the butter in the pan. Let it come to a boil for about ten seconds, then turn off the heat. Set aside for a minute.

In a separate bowl, mix together the buttermilk, eggs, baking soda, and vanilla.

Pour the butter/coffee mixture into the flour mixture. Stir together gently and let cool for a few minutes.

Add in the egg mixture and stir gently until well combined.

Distribute evenly between the 2 cake pans.

Bake for 20 to 22 minutes or until springy to the touch.

Allow to cool completely.

Icing
Place the sticks of butter in a bowl and add in the confectioners' sugar and instant coffee.

Add 2 tablespoons heavy cream and whip mixture together until light and fluffy. You can use an electric mixer if you like. Add in more cream, 1 tablespoon at a time, until it reaches the consistency you want. Don't let it get too wet or it won't stay on the cake.

Spread just under half of the frosting on one half of cake. Place the other half on top.

Spread the remaining icing on the top and around the sides if desired.

Chill for an hour before serving.

Chocolate Coffee Ruin Cake

1 tablespoon water
¼ cup sugar
1 cup dark chocolate in small pieces
1 tablespoon rum, brandy or Grand Marnier
½ pint/300 ml double cream
20 sponge fingers (Boudoir biscuits)
4 fl oz/100 ml strong black coffee
¼ cup grated chocolate

Heat the water and sugar, stirring constantly, until the sugar has dissolved. Leave to cool.

Put the chocolate in a small bowl over a pan of hot water. Heat gently and stir the chocolate as it melts. Turn off the heat as soon as the chocolate is runny.

Add the cooled syrup, stirring constantly.

Stir in the rum, brandy or Grand Marnier and 45 ml/3 tablespoons cream.

Arrange half of the sponge fingers in the bottom of a serving dish. Carefully sprinkle some of the coffee over the sponge fingers, enough to just moisten them. Spread half of the chocolate mixture over the top.

Arrange a second layer of sponge fingers gently over the chocolate. Sprinkle with coffee and spread with chocolate as before.

Whisk the remaining cream until it is just firm. Spread over the top and sides of the cake and chill for 1 hour.

Serve decorated with grated chocolate.

Coffee Carrot Cake

2 cups all purpose flour
2 cups sugar
2 teaspoons baking soda
1 teaspoon baking powder
1 teaspoon salt
1½ teaspoons cinnamon
½ teaspoon allspice
½ teaspoon nutmeg
4 large eggs
2 tablespoons instant coffee or instant espresso powder for stronger flavor
4 cups carrots, finely grated (measure after grating)
1 cup canola oil
1 cup pecans, chopped (measure after chopping)

Heat oven to 350F.
Grease and flour a 13 x 9 inch baking pan.

Mix together the flour, sugar, baking soda, baking powder, salt, and spices.

In a large bowl, beat together the eggs and instant coffee.

Add the flour mixture, carrots, and oil and beat until well blended.

Stir in the nuts. Pour mixture into the prepared baking pan.

Bake for 1 hour until cake tester inserted in center comes out clean.

Cool in the pan for 10 minutes on a wire rack.

Loosen the cake from the sides of the pan with a spatula or knife.

Gently invert the cake onto the rack.

Cool completely.

Frost with Coffee Cream Cheese Frosting or another frosting of your choice.

Espresso Brownies

1 bar espresso-flavored sweet dark chocolate, coarsely chopped (8 oz bar)
1½ sticks unsalted butter
2 tablespoons unsweetened cocoa powder
2 large eggs
1 cup sugar
2 teaspoons vanilla extract
1 cup all purpose flour
¼ teaspoon salt

Preheat oven to 350F.
Grease a 9 inch square baking pan.

Melt the chocolate and butter in a heatproof bowl set over a saucepan containing 1 inch of simmering water.

Remove from the heat, stir in the cocoa powder and let cool.

In a large bowl, beat the eggs for 1 minute.

Add the sugar and beat until the mixture is pale yellow.

Fold in the melted chocolate and vanilla.

Sift the flour over the batter, add the salt and mix until combined.

Spread the batter evenly in the prepared pan.

Bake the brownies for about 45 minutes, or until a toothpick inserted in the center comes out clean.

Let cool before cutting into squares.

Don't eat too fast!

Mocha Mayonnaise Cake

2 cups all purpose flour
1 cup sugar
½ cup cocoa powder
2 teaspoons baking soda
¼ teaspoon salt
1 cup mayonnaise
1 cup cold strong espresso or strong brewed coffee
1 teaspoon vanilla extract

Preheat oven to 350F.
Grease and flour, or line a 13 x 9 inch baking pan.

Sift the flour, sugar, cocoa, baking soda, and salt into a medium bowl and make a well in the center.

In another bowl, whisk the mayonnaise, coffee, and vanilla. Pour into the well.

Mix with an electric mixer on low speed, scraping down the sides of the bowl as needed, just until the batter is smooth; do not overbeat.

Pour the batter into the pan and smooth the top.

Bake for about 30 minutes until a cake tester inserted into the center of the cake comes out clean.

Transfer to a wire cake rack and allow to cool completely.

Spread frosting of your choice over the top of the cake.

Coffee Ginger Muffins

1¾ cups all purpose flour
½ cup sugar
1 teaspoon baking soda
¼ teaspoon salt
¼ teaspoon ground ginger
½ teaspoon ground cardamon
1 large egg
½ cup molasses
½ cup espresso, or strong brewed coffee
¼ cup melted butter

Preheat oven to 375F.
Grease or line with paper, 24 x 2¾ inch muffin cups.

In a large bowl mix together the flour, baking soda, ginger, cardamon, salt, and sugar.

In another bowl beat the egg, molasses, coffee and butter until smooth. Pour into the dry ingredients and stir until just combined.

Fill each muffin cup about ¾ full.

Bake for 15 to 20 minutes until a skewer or cake tester inserted into the center of a muffin comes out clean.

Cool in the pan on a wire rack for 5 minutes before removing to cooling rack.

Walnut Coffee Sandwich

1 cup fine sugar
1 cup softened butter
4 eggs, beaten
2 cups self raising flour
1 teaspoon baking powder
15 walnut halves
2 heaped tablespoons instant coffee,
      dissolved in 1 tablespoon boiling water

Filling
16 oz pot mascarpone cheese
½ cup soft brown sugar
4 tablespoons Kahlua, Tia Maria, or liqueur of your choice such as Bailey's Irish Cream
a few toasted walnut halves, for decoration

Preheat oven to 375F.
Grease and line 2 x 8 inch shallow cake pans.

Toast the walnut halves in the oven for 10 mins. Reserve 10 and chop the rest.

Dissolve the instant coffee in 1 tbsp of boiling water and allow to cool.

In a large bowl, beat all the cake ingredients together until you have a smooth, soft batter.

Divide the mixture between the pans.

Bake for about 20 mins until golden and the cake springs back when pressed.

Turn onto a cooling rack and leave to cool completely.

For the filling, beat the mascarpone with the sugar and liqueur until smooth.

Sandwich the cooled cakes with a third of the filling and the chopped walnuts.

Cover the top and sides of the cake with the rest of the filling and decorate the top with the toasted walnut halves.

Espresso Choc Banana Bread

1½ cups all purpose flour
1½ teaspoons espresso powder
1½ teaspoons baking soda
1 teaspoon salt
1¼ cups very ripe mashed bananas (about 3 large)
¼ cup brown sugar
½ stick butter, melted
¼ cup milk
1 egg
1 cup dark chocolate chips

Preheat the oven to 350 F.
Grease a 9 x 5 inch loaf pan.

In a large bowl mix together the flour, espresso powder, baking soda, and salt.

Beat melted butter and sugar until light and fluffy.

Add the egg, beat for about a minute then beat in mashed bananas and milk.

Add dry ingredients and stir until just combined.

Fold in chocolate chips.

Pour batter into prepared pan and bake for 55-60 minutes, or until a toothpick inserted into the center of the loaf comes out clean.

Let bread cool in pan for 10 minutes before transferring to a wire rack to cool completely.

Coffee Macarons

3 egg whites, kept at room temp for 24 to 48 hours
¼ cup white sugar
2 cups powdered/confectioners' sugar, sifted
1 cup almond flour, sifted
1 tablespoon instant coffee, sifted

Filling:
1 cup chocolate chips
1 tablespoon instant coffee
½ cup heavy whipping cream

*Heat oven later when resting macarons - 300F

Line a baking sheet with parchment paper or baking mat.

Beat the egg whites with the white sugar until peaks form.

Mix together the instant coffee, almond flour and powdered sugar. Stir into the egg whites.

Pour mixture into a piping bag and pipe thick circles onto the baking sheet.

Get rid of air bubbles by tapping on the edge of the baking sheet 3 or 4 times.

Let sit for 20 minutes at room temperature.

Bake at 300F for 12 to 15 minutes until they release easily from the parchment paper or baking mat.

Make the filling:

Warm the whipping cream over a medium heat until it just starts to boil.

Remove from the heat and add the chocolate chips and instant coffee. Let sit for about 30 seconds then stir gently until the chocolate is completely melted.

Let cool to room temperature.

Spread the filling onto the bottom half of one macaron and top with a second, gently squeezing to spread the filling to the edges.

Keep refrigerated until ready to serve.

Coffee Pecan Muffins

1¾ cups all purpose flour
⅓ cup brown sugar
1 tablespoon baking powder
¼ teaspoon salt
1 cup chopped pecans
½ cup butter, melted
¾ cup milk
2 tablespoons instant espresso powder
1 teaspoon vanilla extract
1 egg

Preheat oven to 375F.
Lightly grease 10 muffin cups, or use paper cups in muffin pan.

In a large mixing bowl, combine flour, ⅓ cup brown sugar, baking powder, salt and chopped pecans.

Add melted butter, milk, coffee, vanilla and egg and mix until well combined.

Fill the prepared muffin cups about 2 thirds full.

Bake for 18 to 20 minutes, or until a toothpick inserted into the center of a muffin comes out clean.

Cool in pan for a few minutes and turn out onto wire rack.

Crunchy Coffee Bars

2 cups brown sugar, packed
2 eggs
1 cup butter
1 cup warm coffee
1 teaspoon vanilla extract
3 cups flour
1 teaspoon baking soda
1 teaspoon salt
1½ cups chocolate chips
1½ cups salted peanuts

Preheat oven to 350F.

Combine all the ingredients, except the chocolate chips and the peanuts.

Pour the mixture into an ungreased 13 x 9 inch baking dish.

Top with the chocolate chips and the peanuts.

Bake for 30 minutes.

Allow to cool and cut into rectangles.

Chocolate Espresso Cake

¾ cup butter
¾ cup cocoa powder
1 cup hot espresso or strong brewed coffee
1½ teaspoons vanilla extract
1 teaspoon baking soda
1½ cups Medjool dates (12 to 14), pitted and coarsely chopped
2 cups flour
2 teaspoons baking powder
¾ teaspoon salt
1 cup packed dark brown sugar
2 large eggs

Special equipment: a 9 inch springform pan

Preheat oven to 350F.
Butter springform pan and lightly dust with cocoa powder.

Stir together hot espresso, vanilla, and baking soda in a bowl, then add dates, mashing lightly with a fork, and steep until liquid cools to room temperature, about 10 minutes.

Mix together flour, cocoa powder, baking powder, and salt in another bowl.

Beat together butter and brown sugar until pale and fluffy.

Beat in the eggs one at a time.

Beat in date mixture and add the flour a little at a time, mixing until just combined.

Spoon batter into springform pan, smoothing top, and bake until a wooden pick or skewer inserted into center comes out clean, about 50 minutes to 1 hour.

Cool cake in pan on a rack for 5 minutes, then remove side of pan and cool cake on rack. Serve cake warm or at room temperature.

Moist Coffee Cake

2 cups flour
2 sticks butter
1 cup sugar
2 large eggs
1½ teaspoon baking powder
½ teaspoon salt
½ cup cold strong coffee

For the syrup
⅓ cup hot, freshly brewed espresso
⅓ cup sugar
⅓ cup dark rum or water

Preheat oven to 350F.
Grease and line an 8 inch round cake pan.

Cream the butter and sugar together until light and fluffy.

Beat in the eggs one at a time.

Sift the flour with the baking powder and salt and fold into the mixture with the coffee.

Turn the mixture into the prepared pan and bake for 50 minutes to 1 hour until well risen and firm to the touch.

To make the coffee syrup; in a bowl, stir together the espresso and sugar until the sugar dissolves. Add the rum or water and let cool to room temperature.

Turn the cake out on to a wire rack and prick the surface with a fine skewer.

Pour the coffee syrup over the cake and leave until cold.

Note - Make sure you put the syrup on the cake while it's still warm or it will not be absorbed.

Coffee Banana Nut Muffins

1½ cups all purpose flour
¾ cup sugar
⅓ cup melted butter
4 very ripe bananas, mashed
1 beaten egg
1 teaspoon baking soda
1 teaspoon vanilla extract
1 pinch salt
2 tablespoons strong coffee
1 cup chopped pecans

Preheat oven to 350F.
Grease a 12 cup muffin pan or use paper muffin cups.

In a large bowl beat the butter into the mashed bananas.

Mix in the sugar, egg, coffee and vanilla.

Sprinkle the baking soda and salt over the mixture and stir in.

Add the flour and mix until it is just combined.

Fold in the chopped pecans.

Pour mixture into muffin cups about ⅔ full.

Bake for 20 to 30 minutes. Cool on a rack.

Coffee Madeira Cake

3 sticks unsalted butter
1 cup fine sugar, plus extra for sprinkling
4 tablespoons espresso
1½ cups self raising flour
1 cup all purpose flour, sifted
3 large eggs at room temperature

Preheat the oven to 325F.
Grease and line an 8 inch round cake pan or loaf pan.

Cream the butter and sugar.
Add the coffee and mix well.

Add the eggs one at a time with a tablespoon of the flour for each.

Gently fold in the rest of the flour. If the mixture seems too dry add a little more espresso or a drop of milk.

Sprinkle with fine sugar and bake for 1 hour or until a cake-tester comes out clean.

Place on cooling rack and let cool in the pan before turning out.

Chocolate Espresso Muffins

1⅓ cups all purpose flour
1 stick unsalted butter
⅓ cup unsweetened cocoa powder
1 teaspoon baking powder
½ teaspoon baking soda
¼ teaspoon salt
½ cup whole milk
½ cup strong espresso or strong brewed coffee, cooled
1 teaspoon vanilla extract
½ cup fine sugar
½ cup light brown sugar
1 egg

Preheat oven to 350F.
Line a standard-size muffin pan with paper muffin cups.

Mix together the flour, cocoa powder, baking powder, baking soda and salt.

In a large bowl, beat the butter and both sugars together until light and fluffy.

Add the egg and beat until combined.

Mix the milk, coffee and vanilla together in a jug.

Slowly add a few tablespoons of the flour mixture to the butter and eggs, alternating with the coffee mixture and finishing with the flour mix.

Divide the batter evenly between the 12 muffin cups.

Bake for 17-20 minutes or until a toothpick inserted in the center of a cupcake comes out clean.

Cool completely then top with your choice of frosting.

Coffee Fruit Cake

3 cups mixed dried fruit
1 cup strong brewed coffee
2 sticks butter
⅔ cup brown sugar
1 teaspoon allspice
1 cup self raising, wholewheat, or white flour
1 cup plain wholewheat or white flour
1 teaspoon bicarbonate of soda
2 eggs, beaten

Put the dried fruit in a saucepan with the coffee, butter, sugar and mixed spice.

Slowly bring to the boil and simmer gently for 2 minutes. Remove from the heat and leave to cool for about 1 hour.

Preheat the oven to 350F.
Grease and line an 8 inch round cake pan.

Put the flours and bicarbonate of soda into a mixing bowl.

Add the fruit mixture with the eggs and mix thoroughly until evenly blended. It will be quite sloppy.

Pour into the cake pan and bake for 15 minutes, then lower the temperature to 325F.

Bake for a further 1 hour or until a skewer inserted in the center comes out clean. Turn out onto a wire cooling rack.

Coffee Rice Pudding

1 cup espresso or strong brewed coffee
1 orange, shredded zest and juice
1 cup arborio rice
4 cups milk
4 drops vanilla extract
1 cup sugar
4 tablespoons butter
1 cup heavy cream
4 tablespoons rum (optional)

Put the coffee and orange juice in a saucepan with the coffee and bring to a boil.

Remove from heat, add the rice and let soak for 5 minutes.

Add the milk and vanilla, and cook over low heat until rice is tender, but still slightly firm to the bite.

Remove from heat, add sugar, orange zest, butter, cream, and rum (if using).

Stir through gently and serve at once.

Coffee Creme Brownies

1 (3 ounces) package cream cheese
2 tablespoons butter
¼ cup sugar
4 eggs
½ teaspoon vanilla
1 tablespoon flour
¼ cup warm espresso or strong brewed coffee
1 (19.8 ounces) box family size brownie mix
½ cup vegetable oil

Preheat oven to 350F.
Grease a 9 x 13 inch baking dish.

Put cream cheese and butter into a bowl and beat together with a wooden spoon.

Add sugar and beat until light and fluffy.

Beat in 1 egg and vanilla, then stir in flour and mix well. Set aside.

In another bowl beat together the brownie mix, coffee, remaining 3 eggs, and vegetable oil.

Pour half the batter into the baking dish.

Drop heaped tablespoons of the cheese mixture over the brownie batter.

Pour on remaining batter and gently swirl a butter knife through it to create a marbled effect.

Bake for 25 to 30 minutes.

Mocha Cookies

1 cup butter
3 cups semi sweet chocolate chips
3 tablespoons instant coffee
4 eggs, whisked
1 ½ cups white sugar
1 ½ cups brown sugar
1 tablespoon vanilla extract
4 cups all-purpose flour
⅔ cup cocoa powder
1 teaspoon baking powder
1 teaspoon salt

Preheat oven to 350F.

Melt chocolate chips and butter together in a small pan over a medium heat until smooth. Remove from heat.

Add in the coffee and let stand for 5 minutes.

In a large bowl combine the white sugar, brown sugar and whisked eggs. Stir in the chocolate mixture.

Combine flour and cocoa powder together in a bowl and add to the other ingredients. Stir together well.

Refrigerate for 30 minutes.

Place balls of the cookie dough onto a baking sheet about 1 inch apart.

Bake for 12 to 15 minutes.

Cappuccino Cheesecake Pie with Pecan Sauce

One 10" ready made pie crust
Filling
3 (8oz) packages cream cheese, softened
1¾ cups firmly packed dark brown sugar
4 Eggs
2 tablespoons espresso or strong brewed coffee

Sauce
1 cup firmly packed dark brown sugar
1cup whipping cream
½ cup butter
¼ cup strong coffee
2 tablespoons coffee liqueur or strong coffee
1 cup pecans, chopped

Preheat oven to 350F.

In large bowl, beat cream cheese and brown sugar until smooth.

Add eggs and beat until well blended.

Add 2 tablespoons coffee and blend well.

Pour into crust.

Bake for 45-50 minutes or until edges are set and golden brown (center will not appear set).

Cover edge of crust with strips of foil after 15-20 minutes of baking to prevent excessive browning.

Cool, then refrigerate until thoroughly chilled and center is set, about 2 hours.

Sauce:
In medium saucepan, combine all sauce ingredients except pecans.

Bring to a boil over medium heat, stirring occasionally.

Reduce heat; simmer 5 minutes, stirring occasionally.

Stir in chopped pecans.

To serve, pour warm sauce over each serving.

Garnish with whipped cream and pecan halves.

Boozy Espresso Balls

1 pack chocolate wafers
1 cup skinned toasted hazelnuts
1½ cups confectioners' sugar
2 tablespoons instant espresso powder
½ cup orange liqueur
2½ tablespoons corn syrup
1 cup dessicated coconut

Put the chocolate wafers and hazelnuts in a food processor and pulse until crumbly.

Add the confectioners' sugar and process to combine.

Dissolve the espresso in the orange liqueur and add to the chocolate crumbs along with the corn syrup.

Process until the mixture forms a moist mass.

Put the coconut into a bowl.

Take small pieces of the mixture and roll into 1 inch balls. Roll each ball in coconut and place on waxed paper.

Store loosely packed between layers of waxed paper in an airtight container.

Age for 1 week before serving.
Great with after dinner coffee.

Coffee Cream Cheese Frosting

8 oz softened cream cheese
2 tablespoons softened butter
2 tablespoons strong cold coffee
1 teaspoon vanilla extract
3 cups sifted powdered/confectioners' sugar

Cream the butter and cream cheese together until light and fluffy.

Add the coffee and vanilla; whip until fluffy and smooth.

Add the powdered sugar a little at a time, continuing to whip until all the sugar is added and the frosting is fluffy and creamy.

Add more sugar and coffee if desired.

Coffee Buttercream Frosting

⅓ cup soft butter
1 cup powdered/confectioners' sugar
1 tablespoon instant coffee powder dissolved in a tablespoon of boiling water, or 2 to 3 tablespoons cold strong coffee
few drops vanilla extract

Beat butter and icing sugar until smooth and creamy.

Add coffee and vanilla and beat until blended.

Espresso Buttercream Frosting

2 sticks unsalted butter, softened
2½ cups powdered/confectioners' sugar
1½ teaspoons vanilla extract
1½ teaspoons espresso powder

Mix the espresso powder into the vanilla until dissolved.

Whip the butter and then beat in the sugar until smooth and creamy.

Add the espresso and vanilla mix, and stir until combined.

Makes enough to frost 12 cupcakes or one large cake.

Coffee Fudge Frosting

2 sticks butter
3 tablespoons milk
1lb powdered/confectioners' sugar
2 tablespoons instant coffee powder dissolved in a tablespoon of boiling water, or 2 to 3 tablespoons cold strong coffee
few drops vanilla extract

Put the butter, milk, icing sugar and coffee into a bowl over a pan of boiling water and stir until the mixture is thick.

Remove from the heat and allow to cool until thick enough to spread.

This is enough to sandwich the cake and ice the top.

Chocolate Fudge Frosting

6 ounces unsweetened chocolate, melted and cooled
4½ cups powdered/confectioners' sugar
3 sticks (12 ounces) unsalted butter, at room temperature
6 tablespoons half-and-half or whole milk
1 tablespoon vanilla extract

Place all of the ingredients in a food processor and pulse to incorporate, then process until the frosting is smooth.

Mocha Sour Cream Frosting

4 teaspoons strong brewed coffee
1 cup sour cream
8 ounces bittersweet or semisweet chocolate, chopped into small pieces

Stir the coffee into the sour cream and set aside.

Place the chocolate in a small bowl set over a pan of barely simmering water.

Stir frequently until melted and smooth. Or microwave on medium power for 3 to 4 minutes, stirring from time to time.

Remove from the heat and add the sour cream to the chocolate and stir until just combined.

Use immediately. If the frosting becomes too stiff or loses its gloss, set the bowl in a pan of hot water for a few seconds to soften.

Coffee Glace Icing

1 cup powdered/confectioners' sugar
4 teaspoons water (approx)
1 teaspoon instant coffee

Sift the sugar.

Mix the coffee with 1 tablespoon of water and put into a small saucepan with the icing sugar.

Warm very gently and beat well with a wooden spoon.

The icing should coat the back of the spoon thickly. If it is too thick, add a little water; if too thin add a very little sifted sugar.

Jane's Special Espresso Martini

1 cup cold espresso
1½ shots Van Gogh Double Espresso Vodka
1½ shots Bailey's Irish Cream
Pot heavy whipping cream

Pour ingredients into shaker filled with ice, shake vigorously, and strain into chilled martini glass.

Top with a little heavy cream poured over the back of a spoon if desired, and a little sprinkle of chocolate powder.

Decadent and addictive!

If you have enjoyed this book I would really appreciate it if you would post a review on Amazon.
Thank you so much.
http://www.amazon.com/Recipes-brownie-dessert-recipes-ebook/dp/B008C8W88Y

More books by this author:

Traditional British Jubilee Recipes 4 Book Collection
http://www.amazon.com/Traditional-British-Recipes-Collection-ebook/dp/B00885YZ2I

Traditional British Scones Recipes
http://www.amazon.com/Traditional-British-Scone-Recipes-ebook/dp/B0085EYAZE

Traditional British Cake Recipes
http://www.amazon.com/Traditional-British-Cake-Recipes-ebook/dp/B0084UQB2O

Traditional British Pudding Recipes
http://www.amazon.com/Traditional-British-Pudding-Recipes-ebook/dp/B0085H0LSQ

Traditional British Biscuit Recipes
http://www.amazon.com/Traditional-British-Biscuit-Recipes-ebook/dp/B0085YS9O2

Books for kids:

Little Princess Easy Bake Oven Recipes
http://www.amazon.com/Little-Princess-Easy-Bake-Recipes-ebook/dp/B008JHVOHE

Little Princess Easy Bake Oven Recipe and Coloring Book
http://www.amazon.com/Little-Princess-Easy-Recipe-Coloring/dp/1943828040

Little Dudes Easy Bake Oven Recipes
http://www.amazon.com/Little-Dudes-Easy-Bake-Recipes-ebook/dp/B008JHVQEA

Little Dudes Easy Bake Oven Recipe and Coloring Book
http://www.amazon.com/Little-Dudes-Easy-Recipe-Coloring/dp/1943828059

Printed in Great Britain
by Amazon